The Unreliable Tree

The Unreliable Tree

POEMS

Margot Kahn

Curbstone Books / Northwestern University Press
Evanston, Illinois

Curbstone Books
Northwestern University Press
www.nupress.northwestern.edu

Printed in the United States of America

10 9 8 7 6 5 4 3 2 1

Library of Congress Cataloging-in-Publication Data

Names: Kahn, Margot, 1978– author.
Title: The unreliable tree : poems / Margot Kahn.
Description: Evanston, Illinois : Curbstone Books/Northwestern University Press, 2025.
Identifiers: LCCN 2025016593 | ISBN 9780810148932 paperback | ISBN 9780810148949 ebook
Subjects: LCGFT: Poetry
Classification: LCC PS3611.A35348 U57 2025 | DDC 811.6—dc23/eng/20250408
LC record available at https://lccn.loc.gov/2025016593

O, to take what we love inside,
to carry within us an orchard, to eat
not only the skin, but the shade,
not only the sugar, but the days . . .

—Li-Young Lee

CONTENTS

The Unreliable Tree

I.

MARRYING

My husband and I marry every year
eating apricots from the unreliable tree.
Some years it's only two or three,
while others we have enough for jam
and for eating cold out of hand
barefoot in the kitchen, or leaning
against the sun-drenched side of the house
eyeing the figs and peaches.

I never imagined how inconsequential
we would be, how at the mercy of the wind,
the rain, the bees. I like a place with history,
but of fruit in myth I disagree:
before us, a long marriage lived here.
Listen—it is speaking.

ON A SPRING SUNDAY, I FORGET MY WEDDING RING

and, walking up the hill to the house of my friend,
my naked fingers rub against each other

conscious of that unarmored skin.
My friend stood beside me when I married,

and I stood beside my friend,
and before that we slept in the same bed

laughing about nothing things, like the fact
of whales being mammals and certain tight garments

shimmering. Now I am carrying meatballs in a plastic
bag because, while looking into the face of uncertainty,

my friend must eat. And while I am walking,
a man half my age passes on the sidewalk

and I'm delighted by how my body sings—
it thrums as throaty a song as the warblers

in the soft-lipped magnolia trees. Perhaps
if I hadn't forgotten my wedding ring

where I left it on the counter while mixing
the meat, that man wouldn't have smiled,

and I wouldn't have something
to laugh about with my friend

when I hold her close, our breasts pressed
together, as young and alive as we'll ever be.

NORDSTROM LINGERIE

Each pale pink box the salesgirl brings declares
these breasts were made by hand in Germany,

and we take each one gingerly, hold them
up like paper bags of produce to test

the weight and density, to notice how
the silicone creases like our sad, sagging skin.

And suddenly we're in our high school skins,
palming our nipples and staring like we can't believe

our luck. To find one that matches the breast
that's left, we pass them hand to hand,

the way you separate the raw yolk of an egg.

FIELD OF VISION

Feathery as a frayed hem,
in the wind the hayfield moves
like the tufted manes of a thousand
horses running. No—it moves
like the pleated skirts of a thousand girls
swishing as they walk to school.
After school, there was a girl's field
we'd crouch down in, curl and shiver
like fawns as someone's legs
passed by so close it seemed
impossible they wouldn't find you.
They were tortures in equal
measure: the waiting and
the being found. From the edges
of that field, the girl's father whistled.
There was a whistling tune, and
a sharper sound that brought the children
swift as sheepdogs from the hayfield
or from the fronds of the willow tree,
or from the far fence we'd climb
to watch the neighbor's horses,
pretending they were ours.
Last week at the post office,
the tellers could barely be heard
over the thousand chicks cheeping
in cardboard boxes behind the counter.
Their feathery non-feathers. Their cheeps
of being young in a strange place
with only a small hole to see through.
I didn't do well in school,
but I have come to understand
that a bond is only as strong
as a breath of air. When I learned

that the girl I used to hide with
no longer speaks to her father,
I thought of her room strung up
with 4-H ribbons, their blue and red tails
fluttering against a floral wall.
The hay will be cut tomorrow.
The raptors will come circling.
We'll watch from the shed roof,
where we can see the patterns
the mower cuts in the field.

THE WORLD IN MY PHONE & OUT THE WINDOW

California's in flames.
Hoarfrost lights the fields.

Sexual misconducts tally on.
Fog rises off the water.

Containers wait to set sail.
There's snow all over Brooklyn.

Plovers skim across the Sound.
Logs are sorted for the saw.

A friend's daughter dances in Tel Aviv
barefoot, curly-haired, spinning.

My husband's message arrives: *Is your train on time?*
Someone I've never met has painted her nails red.

ACCIDENTAL HOSTS

We fuck several times a week
until it gets tiresome and then we
watch TV or go to the movies.

If the days don't add up, we
forget about it for the month and
drink with abandon. No matter

if we're supposed to stay away
from queso, street drugs, and raw eggs.
If, in those weeks, our uterine linings

look thin or sad, it's not because we
haven't tried. But we wouldn't say we are
trying. When the baby is conceived

we'll drink only tea. If it's a ghost,
we'll lie down to hold it in
until we have to stand up,

put our hands between our legs
and let it slip through our fingers
down the drain. If the twelfth week comes

and it's still there, we will make phone calls
and fill out paperwork. We are not puppets
or disciples. We don't want to be cast out,

marooned with a crib in an empty room.
We are accidental hosts. We want to be
what we've been—go to the same job,

the same bar, shoot the same game of pool
when our stomachs bulge over the lip
of the table. We are reviled, derided,

feared, and crowned. Yes, some fit
in their regular jeans for six months
and don't break out and still want sex,

but look—look at this thing we've done
because we're animals and we said,
We'll see what happens until

it actually happens and we find ourselves
standing in the light of the open door
peeling deli meat from the paper wrapping,

folding it into our mouths.

PRECAUTION

In the waiting room for mammography,
there's a ginger-haired mermaid with breasts

bare and round as the moon. She belongs
in Marseille, dark hands against the sea,

not here holding an armload of peonies.
All the other women in this waiting room

are old and as far as I'm concerned may die—
their children can feed themselves dinner.

On the way home, lilacs drip and shiver
above my head. The scent fills my chest

with feathers. If only I could flip a switchblade
open with my thumb, cut each breast cleanly,

hang them in the tree, let my nipples peek out
from among the purple flowers.

MY MOTHER COULD ALWAYS WEAR ANYTHING

A friend calls, says, *I need to start*
loving my body. We laugh when she says,
If not now, when?

In the yard, the dog sleeps
with her legs splayed wide,
the fir cone tuft of her vagina

pointing straight to the sky.
When the package truck arrives,
the driver hands her half a Milk-Bone

and crouches down, delivers
a blue envelope I'll tear
open later. When my mother

was here she put her feet
on the coffee table, revealed
her muddled ankles,

dark stains of blackberries,
her legs peppered with divots
like my two-rut drive.

It'd been two years
since I'd seen her.
I can't wear shorts anymore,

she'd said. My svelte,
off-the-shoulder
mother, her legs

always the envy.
After she went to bed,
I went online and ordered

these cotton canvas shorts
the custard color of lemon bars
and the barn's star

and the light in London
at four in the morning
coming out of a club,

the kind where I used to wear silver
trousers and moonlit velvet
shirts without sleeves.

COLD CREEK

These are the last days of spring snow.
We take advantage by strapping on skis

and going out Cold Creek where the firs
drop veils of snow as we pass beneath.

I've read that the Germans have a word
for forest solitude, and another for forest obscurity.

Do they have a word for crossing a bridge?
For the feeling in your arms and legs

when you have, possibly, ventured too far?
Do they have a word for the tracks

a creature leaves dimpled in the snow,
those empty pockets of shadow?

At the warming hut, the wood stove's heat
shimmers and yawns. Someone offers

hot buttered rum steaming in a steel cup,
cheese and crackers, and sweet, dried mango

that sticks in the crannies of our teeth.
On the way back, our knees ache.

Make it burn, I say, and we laugh
about it, the aching. Is there a word

for the living thing that once was here
and now is not? The wind and sun

will take care of its footprints.

AN OPENING

The wind is blowing across the freshly plowed field,
its raw ropes of furrows and its little creatures—

earthworms, cutworms, wireworms, slugs.
The wind blows up the road through the madrones

and cedars, shakes the catkins and rattles the tired
old rose hips in the hedgerows' thorny arms.

It brings gold dust to sift across the back porch,
the black chairs, the blue car.

Coming up from Barney's pond, the wind brings
the frogs' night song, the tanker's horn, the sparrows'

morning briefing. It brings the salty brine of low tide,
the sharp tang of snow, and a memory of driving

to the mountains in early fall, the ranger warning
if snow fell we'd be stuck 'til spring. The wind

snapped the thin sheet of our tent all night
while we tried to sleep, and the small bag

of provisions swayed from its rope in the trees.
When we woke, it was to a pink sky

and the late-summer flowers, paintbrush and lupine—
the wind cold against our cheeks.

WESTERN TANAGER

Arriving in woodlands in the middle of May,
he's redheaded and yellow-cloaked—dashing!

And you, wearing your new breast, your legs
iridescent as a hummingbird, your head

as bare as our babies' were, those tender skulls
in the palms of our hands—you're pale now.

Soon the children will be sent away, and you'll
burn and peel and burn. By November

this joule of a bird will have flown. But today—
look at us! stopped on our path, breathless.

II.

PLUM SEASON

In plum season we stand in the latticed
arms of our trees, pick fruit to burnish

against our jeans. Root stock and tender flesh,
these trees were planted by someone else's

ancestors. But then, who isn't living
in diaspora? Who visits the graves

of their old people? Do your people have graves?
Do you even know their names? In the yard,

a Garry oak marks a grave for me to grieve
some other girl's dead dog while, in a country

far away, police have assumed the house
of my grandfather. On the sidewalk,

schoolchildren stop to learn who once lived there.
To think these trees are mine—I have learned nothing.

EXILE

When everything here is up in flames,
I yearn for a yard I know the edge of,

for lightning bugs trapped in a punched-lid jar.
I yearn for the days I got myself to school

and picked myself up, hot-wired the minivan,
got felt up, and learned about loneliness

from a phone that was attached to the wall.
Now, two thousand miles away, the hills

are first to disappear. Then goes the fence,
the garden, the rutted gravel drive. My lungs

hurt just watching, then reading the note
a friend posts—a few bags packed and a quick snap

as they're rushing away, a transcendental
image for an Instagram age. The blur

of the hill behind their house awash in light—
        ablaze.

A QUIET DAY WITH THE WEST ON FIRE

Upstairs, my boy hums while he plays.
Inside a Mason jar, a caterpillar rests
on the branch of a plum tree.

Cake sits on the counter. Bread cools.
A tomato ripens even as we hold
our breath waiting for the wind and rain.

We've asked ourselves the same question
a thousand times. In these days of smoke
and haze, I hold on to the smallest things—

watch the caterpillar sleep, listen
            to the boy sing.

FERMATA

Do you know what that means? says my son, kicking his legs
beneath the piano keys. His arms outstretched don't yet reach
the lowest A or the highest C, but at least he's learning.

In my grandparents' living room I tinkered, never taught,
while my grandmother lit candles for everyone she'd lost.
There, the old people kept the old country to themselves.

Here, the old people lift a finger or two off the steering wheel,
sometimes a whole hand. When I take a turn I hesitate,
questioning whether the wave or the road is more important.

When I was my son's age, my grandmother put a knife
through her palm trying to separate a pair of frozen steaks.
She called for help as if announcing a five-spade hand.

LIGHT IN THE HAND

I wish I remembered the lipstick shade
my grandmother used to wear. Racy Pink?

Hot Tamale? Ooh La La? Bare Beige Cinque?
In the clamshell mirrors her compact made,

light in the hand as a dollar's change, she'd
pull color across her flaccid lips—think

pickled peppers in a steel dish. She'd drink
and leave color on the glass, say something

against love, give me a kiss. What a gift,
those tubes, gold and spiraling. Color to suffuse

the darkness. Forget what's gone and unscrew
a luxury, a change of face. If you had once

lost everything, which color would you choose?
Viva Glam? Ardent Sand? Rouge Rendez-Vous?

DINNER

In attendance: Joel, Jacob,
and Becalel. Mendel, Inda, Shifra.
Great-grandma Gitla. And sickly Chaim,
who committed suicide on the train.
Just my grandfather's mother's side.

The uncles have fish in butter sauce.
The women take steak rare with sides
of greens. Chaim has a breadbasket,
the fifty-dollar pinot, and the vegetable terrine.

For dessert, Shifra orders crème brûlée.
Under the table, Don finds her femur.
He's disgusting, but she giggles—
the gas has made her giddy. *They stink,*
Nick says to Don. *How'd they even get in here?*

Gitla suggests a walk.
The wind chops up the water.
A light rain washes some dirt
from their bones. Underfoot
the clipped grass feels good and cool.

How was the fish, Mendel? Gitla asks.
He says not half bad. *And the steak?*
Overdone. Nevertheless, she says
they should come back.

ELECTROENCEPHALOGRAM

Twenty wires attached to your head,
you're eight seconds gone and [   ] again
licking your lips, rubbing your thumbs to forefingers.

Oh, sweet boy. Where have you been?
Cold room, green lines, the score
of your brain's song on a screen—

tracks missing beneath the train,
the one [   ],
and all the books we took years to read—

every other page removed,
every other scene.

When we walked [   ]
did you see [   ]?

Or was it for you only holes in the tree?
Sweet boy, I'll pick every blade [   ]
you missed, collect every flutter of wings.

THE CLEANER

Years ago, I hired a woman to help me clean.
She would text me during the week
when she was able to come, in between
her other jobs that were haphazard
and unpredictable. Her job that paid real money
was for the city: when there was a body—
a crime scene—she was the one who cleaned it.
And she loved this job, she told me. She loved
knowing which way the bullets flew
and with what velocity the body shattered.

She'd come to my house with Q-tips
and cleaning products she'd made by hand
and tell me everything while I held my baby:
The way blood decorates a wall.
How far splintered bone can travel.
The way scraps of fat and tissue settle
into thick carpet, and what it takes
to find them, pluck them out with tweezers.

One week it was a man who shot himself
in the basement. One week a seventeen-year-old
who hung himself in the garage.
Someone found them, and then someone called her—
my cleaner—to make it disappear
so that when the mother of that boy came home again
she wouldn't find a drop of him:
not a vestige of his smell, not a scrap
of bitten fingernail. Which makes me wonder
what that mother thought would become of her boy
when her boy was young, or what I might feel,
seven years from now, if my son were
to leave this world by his own hand.

Today, on the toilet while I pee,
I stare at the hair on the floor
where my husband gave my son a trim
and wonder if I should keep it—
this clipping that escaped the broom.

THE TOWELS

Above the clawfoot tub they drape
the way the user left them:

my husband's stretched across two hooks
the way a certain kind of man takes up space;

my son's hung up as if entangled,
a foot caught in a stirrup when the rider

has gone down; and mine—
the plush weight of itself folding over.

I take them, bundled in my arms,
ten thousand fiber fingers that go

to the places I do not or can no longer go:
the crease of my son's thigh where a mole

like a button I want to press grows,
and all the crannies of my husband

I still wish to ravish. I clutch them
the way my grandmother bundled

and carried me to bed, where the towel
unfurled at my feet like the loose petal

of a spent flower—the way, she said,
the rotten clothes fell from her cousins' bodies

when the soldiers found them in the forest,
came to tell them the war was over.

ODE TO TRICHOTILLOMANIA

At the dining room table with toast
and tea, I worry the thin hairs that frame
my forehead, my vellus hairs and lashes,
any errant brows. The mailman has surely
seen me, and anyone with whom I've lived,
gather them on my empty plate—
my follicle nests, my inedible
anxious tumbleweeds.

I've heard there's a room of hair at Auschwitz—
hair in piles on the floor. And though I am embarrassed
by this mess I make, you'd have to shave my head,
cut off my hands to make me stop the pleasure
of each pull—the miracle of each root
removed to which I say *grow again.*

FREE BOAT AT THE CORNER OF KJARGAARD AND FISHERMAN BAY

Yellowed tooth keeled to the cows, she's a boat
in a field not far from the sea. You'd think

someone would want her. Water glimmers
in the distance. Cows graze the tender green.

Money hole. Joy ride. The mind sees what it wants
to remember: cold envelope of the ocean,

traps lowered to unlit depths. Who was she
before she got here? Who was I?

What if you took everything you owned
and looked at it against the bareback sky?

I like that I'm a woman who can still
be curious when she turns a corner.

The boat has become a page of the field
that rewrites itself every season.

III.

PRACTICE AT THE COMMUNITY COURTS

They play the court
in staccato slams

and good, long
backhands.

Skirts: short.
Ponytails: swing.

On the path, a man
holds a girl by the wrist

until she stands before him,
until she submits.

Now I am ashamed.
Stay away from Mr. Marsh,

the older girls always said.
The gym teacher. Of course.

But no one talked about
the physics teacher

who got someone pregnant,
or the math teacher

who slept with my best friend.
I watch the girls from outside

the fence where the camellia
and witch hazel

stick their petal tongues
out to the wind.

I wore those skirts once,
let men look at me.

Now I stand with my son
and I cannot look away.

AUGUST

Someone's Corvette is parked on their shag rug lawn,
and the scent of cheap body spray, the kind

a boyfriend wore in high school, spills across the yard.
Sometimes I don't want to like what I do.

The sun sets over the rocks breaching
against the waves, and the blackberries,

cut to the ground last year, are lush again
and flowering. Soon the fruits will be dark

and sweet, and people will swarm to pick them.
Everyone thinks this dead end, this end of the road

is theirs. When the sunlight turns the stop sign
into a flare of light, it's time to go home.

The mosquitoes have come out and the bats slingshot
over my head in a way that makes me queasy,

knowing the heat of me is heard but not seen.

MIXED FEELINGS ABOUT MY CONTRIBUTION TO HUMANITY

There are days in the fall when
on the paths through the park

slugs everywhere are crossing.
I come upon them stretched out

to their longest lengths,
trailing their cursive tracks,

and I stop, stoop, and pick them up,
their soft, wet bodies contracting.

I set them down gently on the other side,
in the new grass

or the soft, dead leaves.
And then there are other days—

days we've been late to school
because none of the clean pants

are comfortable, because
a fraction of toast

has been left on the plate
but cannot be cleared.

Days when doors have been slammed
or books held open, and I am tired

of asking for socks and shoes,
tired of wondering over the whereabouts

of rain boots.
On these days, I get to the park

and see the biker
skimming down the path,

the dog's damp nose, his slip
of indiscriminate tongue,

and I don't stop. I look at the slugs
and say to each one of them,

Good luck, buddy.
Good fucking luck.

AFTER A MASS SHOOTING

Talking to a friend
I am so sad, she says, *I can't—*

a call comes in.
My child is hitting

other children
the schoolteacher says

and I must pick him up
no, not later—now.

At the school, the door
buzzes open, then locks

with a warped
and heavy sound. It is

just before lunch,
and the children

in their classrooms
are sitting down to pray.

The phone rings again.
My brother is getting married.

Another brother
is the best man.

What would I like
to eat: steak

or steelhead trout?
In the car, on the radio,

the sheriff says this tragedy
was not preventable,

that the mind of a madman
is impossible to predict.

The sheriff says,
It will take us days,

months, years to recover.
One hard-boiled egg,

yolk thumbed out,
two mandarin oranges,

and a cream cheese
sandwich, crusts

removed, are snug
in the compartments

of the metal lunch box
we carry home together.

ON THE BUS THROUGH OREGON

A banner of geese unfurls,
cut loose from bolted storm clouds.

Stray snags and burnt cartilage
erupt out of backyards,

loneliness jackknifed
toward a too-bright light.

A freight of peonies goes north,
aching open and broken down.

In all other directions:
brushfire, burn piles.

I'm no one's mother here,
yarn around my fingers,

oranges at my feet.
But I am a promise

of return: mother
as antidote to that lawn

where a hundred missiles
are arranged in lines,

aimed at nothing,
aimed at the sun.

IN WHICH I EXCUSE FREDDY MERCURY FROM P.E.

All year he'd been standing in the hallway
to the pool, the painted lines around his eyes

growing more and more lonely, and the voice
in his throat growing low and soft like

a kitten done mewling for milk,
grown into a new way of living.

In the hall the boy swayed gently
from side to side, like a pine in a stand

of pines at the edge of a coastal city.
He looked at me imploringly.

All he did was look at me.
A long time ago, I was his friend

because he loved me, and that love stayed tender
even though we'd become different creatures.

But the note was a kind of love. The forgery.
I held a piece of paper up against the lockers,

wrote in my best cursive: *Please excuse*
Freddy from swimming today. I wanted

to say, *He does not feel like undressing.*
He does not feel like ruining his makeup.

They wanted him to peel off his clothes,
get in the water, and put his head under

where other boys' feet and legs, their elbow knobs
and knees, would kick and punch to hold afloat

their glistening torsos, their ribs inside
goose-bumped skin. The lines applied

around his eyes would bleed
like the inky whisper of a giant squid.

The water would go dark, the whole
natatorium. The principal's office.

The car ride home, where our mothers—
the same age that I am now—

would not speak to the confusion of their sorrows.
In the principal's office, they made me say,

I'm sorry. But I wasn't sorry then,
and I'm not sorry now. The permission

I gave might have been a lie. But look,
I gave it anyway.

RANCHO BAR

You'll feel like you're on a ship, belowdecks,
my brother says when he takes me to a bar

at the foot of the San Gabriel Mountains.
The ceiling is low. The floor is a carpet of tartan.

It takes three beers and twenty years
for my brother to tell me what he has to say,

show me the pictures of his life scrolling
across a screen. What else have I missed

that's been right before my eyes? Who else
have I not known for the sin of not seeing?

What did you want when you were young?
my brother asks me. *Sex*, I say. I wanted

to travel. *What did you want?* I ask back.
When the rain breaks, we walk home.

From the kitchen you can see all the way
across the valley to Los Feliz,

Sunset, Hollywood, the ocean.
In the bathroom, paper towels in a jar

catch drips from the leaky faucet.
In the bedroom, my brother is sleeping.

What he wanted is still what he wants,
the thing that makes everything easier.

AFTER A WINTER STORM

A man sits on the bus stop bench outside
Bailey-Boushay. He's rocking front to back,

hands gripping his head at each forward fall,
while someone stands over him demanding

something while digging through a plastic bag.
We sit at the light on our way to school,

and I wonder what my son, tucked in his seat
behind me, sees. I think of that man's mother.

The light turns and I've formulated
empathy lessons in my head but have said

nothing. Then we're at the school gate and
it's Valentine's Day. We carry a bag full of hearts

folded and sealed with stickers and tape.
There will be a party with treats and paper-

bag mailboxes. Later, we'll sit at home
on the brown wool rug, the detritus

of the day spilled out before us in shards
of sugar and ink, shaky love letters,

blue-eyed kittens torn and cast aside.
I'll ask my son if I might have a piece,

a peppermint, maybe—something sweet
and sharp at once.

IF SOMEONE SAYS CATALINA

I think of this one low-slung,
corduroy-wearing, cello-playing boy.

His gold hair swung like Janis Joplin's,
like a tiki bar curtain, the fringe

of a flapper dress across my leg.
Together in a twin bed

I was a window
and that hair was a shade

and the tassel, from my neck
to my navel, pulled itself down.

That boy played like nothing
I could afford—a twenty-year

whiskey on the rocks, the melt
of a glacier pooled at my feet.

Now someone says Catalina
or cello or cancer

and I'm there again
singing over his requiem.

Tassel and tongue.
Shade and shroud.

Was it the hair, or the hands?
The sound, or the shape of the sound?

I'm saying this so that you
help me remember him,

so his mother knows
that night is accounted for.

WALKING TO THE END OF THE ROAD ON THE LAST DAY OF JULY

This morning I found wild plums growing
at the end of the road beside the empty-
windowed barn, cool planets in the trees,
and a white-haired woman riding a lawn
mower at the house with the red poppies,
next to the house of the summer people
with their concrete wall and metal fence,
their posted signs: Keep Out, KEEP OUT.

Today the tide is so low it's exposed
islands I've never seen, and tonight
there'll be a black moon, my father-in-law
tells me. It's blackberry season. All the way
home from the end of the road, I pluck
the tender nubs from their vines
wondering about the bay beyond that wall,
the water I imagine to be more tranquil,
more pristine. How have I never noticed
the plums in all the years I've walked to the sea?

IV.

TAKING ADVANTAGE OF A SUMMER'S DAY

I stay in the kitchen, beat salt and butter
with a wooden spoon, go out only to see the beets

in flower before the root has fully grown,
and the poppies' silken petals

flung wantonly open. Why didn't I sit
outside today? Why didn't I move

three feet into the sun? I see the boys
come to cut the tall grass in the septic field,

a raptor's shadow across the lawn.
I am bleeding again, a shattered window,

the bread risen, ready to turn.
There's always another day, until

tomorrow it's supposed to rain. Then I think
about how much I've wasted. Up all night

with the baby, fog hiding the moon
and the field and the barn. I watch it wrap

around the windows, leaden with regret,
and still—by supper we have a string-band

sunset, hummingbirds come to feast
on the zinnias I planted at dawn.

MORNING REVERIE

No one told me to sow my oats.
I did anyway. On a deserted beach
in Maine, blanket on the sand.
Against a sink that fell off the wall
in a yellow bathroom in Brooklyn.
In a mirrored room outside London
where morning crumpets left butter
dripping down our chins.
I have to think of those days now,
married fifteen years, as I consider
the cold film and globules
crusted to the oatmeal pot—
the one left in the sink,
half full of water, "soaking."
Miracle, from the Latin
miraculum: object of wonder.
And meal: to crush, to grind.
What a miraculous crushing, this!
What a fine grind. Some days
I turn my back to the sink
and peel a boiled egg.
Other days, I yield—
pull the rough side of the sponge
across the stainless steel
and slip what's left from the lip of the pot
into the rubber drain's pliant maw.

WANTING

I want a man whose hands have been inside
another man, a still-warm animal.

I want to taste the gun's cold barrel
on his lips, the place that speaks after thinking

of not speaking. I know what it's like
leaving fruits behind: at the fence's edge

shadow holes gape like hungry mouths—a red
rash of flesh bitten to the leafy quick

or half-hinged and pungent as jam
dissolving in June's perennial sun.

How many rotten things have been born of my
imprecision? I'm torn between guilt and triumph

to see a neck snap, to taste
the sweet false taste of conquest.

IN THE ARMOR COURT

In the armor court of my youth, a knight my size
rode a bay in silver chains, and I looked up at her

every Saturday, my stockinged legs and saddle
shoes splayed on the floor like wings.

In the faded scenes that hung from the walls,
women's faces furrowed and frowned, stags

locked with twisted horns, and every now and then
a unicorn walked through a field of flowers.

Gorget, pallette, breastplate, jambeau. Now,
out my window, the paint horse is pissing

with her tail held high, the way a lady flares
her pinkie drinking a dainty cup of tea.

Poleyn, skirt of tasses, solleret, cuisse.
Between us, the hedgerow has put on her studded

pearls. There's one lone bulb in the barn,
and the sky's a museum. From my garden,

picking the turnips and the winter kale, I hear
the girls galloping. The ground sends the sound

before they flay the field. And suddenly
I'm swooning. My whole life I've wanted

to be that girl—plated, chained, impenetrable.
To take the field first, to reveal myself later.

BEFORETIMES

When I run into an ex on the way
to the DMV, it's fall,
or maybe spring, I can't say,

but it's one of those days you go
back to school, or skip school in some small
revolt. He's wearing a white T-shirt and oh

if I'm telling the whole story, you'll
have to know he looks a hell of a lot
better than when we dated, so I'm all

having a moment, questioning my past
decisions, the spiral of my life,
on Eighth Avenue between Fourth and Fifth Street,

and the fact that maybe part of why
I dumped him had to do with the red Chevy
festooned with plastic animal figurines—

the dash, the hood, and the shelf behind the back seats
where in a taxi you'd find a box of Kleenex—
you'd see it and think *Who drives that beast?*

Those were the days of grunge, before the tech
when we all still said hi. There was a naked
parade and no one wore a skin suit—dicks

and tits hung loose, flapping in the wind
as the cyclists cruised the route up Thirty-Fourth
through the neighborhood where I lived,

where D and I lay on a futon and laughed
exploring each other's orifices
like dogs, shamelessly, used every word to ask

And this? And now? And there were pieces
of love but it wasn't love—it was the right
thing for the moment. And now, in all senses,

it's some real universe bullshit
that we're living ten blocks apart
and, since he has the day off, he comes to sit

with me on a bench at the DMV
in a windowless basement in Brooklyn.
While we're there, half the day, he tells me

he's in love with someone named Esther.
Years later, he'll marry her. But on this day,
we sit in that room and play cards together

while I slip my papers in the half-moon tray
and take a number, wait for someone
behind the bulletproof glass to say

take another. And I feel only love.
I don't remember the fear of that year,
or the fear of the years that hover

before and after. I remember
the windowless room and, outside, all
the free books on the steps of stoops, flowers

in buckets at the bodega, his arms
where the shirt stops and the skin begins,
the ziggurats of oranges—the way

I buy some and carry them home
carelessly, in a flimsy plastic bag.

DURING THE PANDEMIC, I GIVE YOU A HAIRCUT

Out on the back porch I'm reminded
of all the twenty-dollar Supercuts

I long ago disparaged. Then a decade
of pricey trims that kept your balding pate

in style. Now it's me you're left with.
You stand a step below to level us.

Start at the nape, you say, *slowly*
so it doesn't yank. Fade to the top,

then go from the bottom up with the two-blade.
I hold the taloned guard, flip the switch

that makes it quiver. In your younger years
someone pulled her fingers through your hair.

No doubt the birds will find this treasure.

ON DISSOLUTION

Behind the old barn
the blackberries crowd
around the water tank,
climb the west wall,
take back the field
along the fence line.
Barney's barn, unused
for decades—listing.
House of bats, house
of owls, house of cats,
house of swallows.
We pick the berries,
muddle them with mint,
shake them with lemon
and vodka, pour
them into pint jars,
and take them in sweet-
bitter sips while
the swallows—bank, barn,
rough-winged, violet-green—
come barnstorming.
They glide in circles
or close to the ground,
slip through the hayloft doors,
through the holes in the roof
and walls that widen each winter
without remorse. This, we agree,
is the solution to dissolution:
alight in the places that will hold you.
Pass through darkness
with the swiftest grace.

INTO THE O.R.

Cold hall, blue room—
more hands, more faces
hover, tend, and loom

than any other place
you've been at the center—
decked in wedding-gown lace,

bat mitzvah, birth, tender
birth of your son, birthdays—
you've not had to surrender

on any other Thursday
to so many hands as today. Legs
strapped, you're a mermaid—

while around the bed
the nurses and nurses' aides
surround your head

moving the way
a shoal of herring
turns all its tails

in sync, sharp and unerring
as the knife to come.
Now, the nurse is asking—

where do you want to go
in your anesthetized mind?
An ocean aglow,

phosphorescent and wild—
the kind you'd never dive
into in all the days you've been alive

before but swear, if you survive,
you will, if you breathe
another year or five—

POST-OP

Clean linens and a string of bells to ring.
They say ten days, two weeks I should chill,

lay low, lie prone, veg out, curl up, unwind,
take it easy. I close my eyes for hours,

thankful to sleep, to dream other versions
of myself that could be *doing*. It's hard

to think the body works even as I lie
still—how it's possible to fix a thing

without lifting a finger. I stare
at the wainscoting: when I'm better

I'll repaint. Blood pools at my hip, yolk-yellow
bruise. Red tulips, cold coffee on the sill.

The other night it hurt so much to cry
I cried. And I see now how pain

could destroy us. It could be you in agony
and me losing sympathy. Or it could be me

sailing out on the solo voyage I've feared
my whole life. I still fear it, but my knives

are sharper: guilt of the wasp, regret
of the rabbit, failure, failure. I ask

for eggs scrambled with butter, a hand
to pull me up and another to lower me down.

WINTER

My husband and I get divorced
every winter, driving over the mountains.
It's like the joke about the chicken,
where the thing on the other side
is something worth getting to, only
the chicken is carrying the Talmud.
We'll be fine, says my husband.
But it's not us, I say,
that I'm worried about.
On the icy road we stop
behind a single-file line of cars.
While we wait, my son tiptoes
to the shoulder and pees.
He is still so young the danger
does not occur to him. The road
is slick under packed snow,
dirty and deceptive,
the way it was when I was young
and boys would take me out in cars
late on winter nights,
crank the wheels and slam
the brakes in empty four-ways,
spinning us like teacups
at the county fair,
flesh smashed into flesh,
careening past tree trunks
and telephone poles, our tires
leaving great, looping,
spirographic tracks
we'd get out to admire,
howling like idiots
in the blank suburban night.

When we push north,
we pass the accident—
the van on its roof, the driver's
side smashed in. The dull wail
of the ambulance coming down valley,
its sad song made soft by the snow.
My grandfather believed God chose him
to survive the Holocaust so he would father
a son. But I am my mother's daughter
and I have no such hubris. I'm here
by dumb luck and despite
this foolishness.
The world outside
is impossible to control,
every damn molecule bonding
and breaking without telling you.
I trusted those boys the way I trust
my husband, his steady hands—
because I have to.

SKIING

We love our children the way the snow
piles on fence posts, the way the plow

comes to clear the drive. We love them
the way the dog bounds away and returns,

ice clinging to its chest, ice frozen
in its paws, hurting. We love our children

and we don't love them, a thing
we can't say unless we're out here

where the tree with the yellow bark
is sending its shooters to the sky,

and the snow's doing that thing it does,
lolling over the lips of things like a dog's

tongue, ice dripping off smooth edges
like saliva. The snow lets our feet slip

away from the house
and along the river, the river

that's saving breath for itself.
We ski past the country store,

past the warming hut, deeper
and deeper into the trees.

ACKNOWLEDGMENTS

Grateful acknowledgment is made to the editors of the following publications, in which these works first appeared, sometimes in different forms:

Catamaran: "Rancho Bar"

Crab Creek Review: "On Dissolution," "The Towels," and "Winter"

Grist: "Fermata"

Hopkins Review: "In the Armor Court"

Jabberwock Review: "The World in My Phone & Out the Window"

Mantis: "Light in the Hand" and "An Opening"

Mom Egg Review: "After a Winter Storm"

New England Review: "Field of Vision"

New Ohio Review: "Exile"

The New Yorker: "Beforetimes"

Nimrod: "Cold Creek"

Poetry Northwest: "Nordstrom Lingerie" and "On a Spring Sunday, I Forget My Wedding Ring"

Pontoon: "Accidental Hosts" and "After a Mass Shooting"

Portland Review: "A Quiet Day with the West on Fire"

San Antonio Review: "If Someone Says Catalina"

Shenandoah: "In Which I Excuse Freddy Mercury from P.E."

Taproot: "Walking to the End of the Road on the Last Day of July"

"During the Pandemic, I Give You a Haircut" appeared in *The New York Times* Letters from Our Readers section ("Coronavirus Poems to the Editor: 'Death Too Wears a Mask' ") on May 20, 2020. It is anthologized in the ebook edition of *Alone Together: Love, Grief, and Comfort During the Time of COVID-19* (Central Avenue Publishing, 2020).

"Accidental Hosts" is after Diane Seuss.

The title of "During the Pandemic, I Give You a Haircut" is after Rick Barot's chapbook *During the Pandemic.*

Some of these poems appeared in the chapbook *A Quiet Day with the West on Fire*, published in 2021 as the finalist of Floating Bridge Press's John Pierce Chapbook Competition.

I learned much of what I know about poetry from *The Poet's Handbook* by Mary Oliver, *How to Read a Poem and Fall in Love with Poetry* by Ed Hirsch, *The Art of Voice* by Tony Hoagland, and *The New Yorker* poetry podcast hosted by Kevin Young. I mention these resources both in gratitude and as an offering to anyone who finds themselves, as I did, on the precipice of a new genre, a little lost and alone, wanting to be a better writer and reader.

Thank you to Laura Read for the 2018 reading in Missoula, Montana, that spurred me to write my very first poem; to Ellen Bass, for the most serendipitous cab ride of my life and subsequent oodles of good advice; to Keetje Kuipers, my first best teacher; and to Erin Malone, whose edits on this manuscript were indispensable.

Thanks to Rick Barot, Ellen Bass, Kendra DeColo, Keetje Kuipers, Danusha Lameris, Dorianne Laux, Erin Malone, and Tess Taylor, in whose classes many of these poems were born, and to Kary Wayson for giving an early draft of this manuscript a careful read. I'm grateful to Sandy Bishop, who rented me a quiet office at just the right time. Thank you, Juniper Blomberg, for taking care of T while I wrote. Thank you, Rebecca Hoogs, Katie Prince, and Sonya Schneider, for your friendship and poetry conversation. Marisa Siegel and the team at Northwestern University Press, thank you for believing in this book and bringing it into the world with such care. Thank you to my family—parents, brothers, aunts, cousins, and especially S & T—for the cookies, hugs, texts, and notebooks. And thank you to the lights of my every-other-weeks: Rebecca Clarren, John Okrent, and Ed Skoog—these poems wouldn't be what they are without you three.